0

zero

нуль
nul

10

ten

десять
desiat

20

twenty

двадцять
dvadtsiat

30

thirty

тридцять
trydtsiat

40

forty

сорок
sorok

50

fifty

п'ятдесят.
p'iatdesiat.

60

sixty

шістдесят
shistdesiat

70

seventy

сімдесят
simdesiat

80

eigthy

вісімдесят

visimdesiat

90

ninety

дев'яносто

dev'ianosto

100

one hundred

сто

sto

1000

one thousand

одна тисяча

odna tysiacha

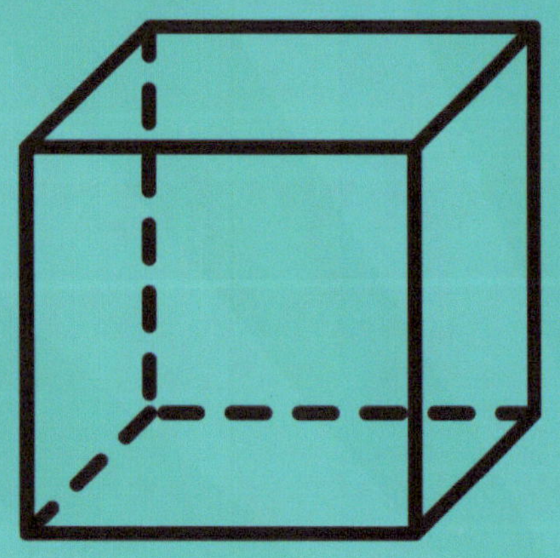

cube

куб
kub

block

блок
blok

ice cube

кубик льоду
kubyk lodu

caramel

карамель
karamel

sugar

цукор
tsukor

dice

гральні кості

hralni kosti

gift box

подарункова коробка

podarunkova korobka

cardboard box

картонна коробка

kartonna korobka

sphere

сфера
sfera

ice cream scoop

ложка для морозива
lozhka dlia morozyva

pearl

перлина
perlyna

bubble

бульбашка
bulbashka

marbles

кульки
kulky

planet

планета
planeta

snowball

сніжок
snizhok

tennis ball

тенісний м'яч
tenisnyi m'iach

cylinder

циліндр
tsylindr

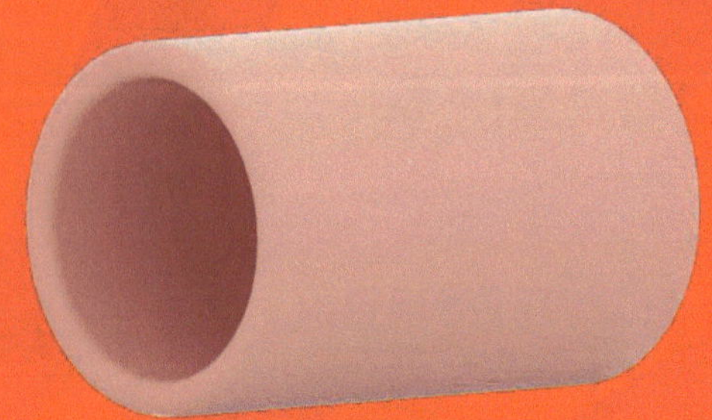

tube

трубка
trubka

batteries

батарейки
batareiky

thread spool

котушка ниток
kotushka nytok

cinnamon

кориця
korytsia

rolling pin

качалка
kachalka

sausage

ковбаса
kovbasa

hay bale

тюк сіна
tiuk sina

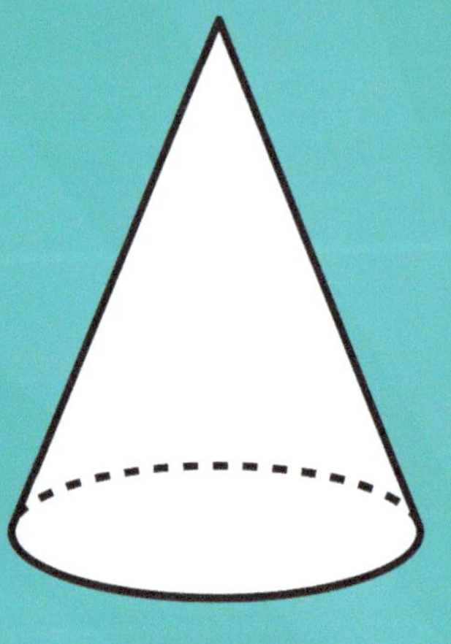

cone

конус

konus

road cone

дорожній конус

dorozhnii konus

ice cream cone

ріжок морозива

rizhok morozyva

witch hat

капелюх відьми

kapeliukh vidmy

dungeon

підземелля

pidzemellia

fir tree

ялинка

ialynka

party hat

капелюх для вечірки

kapeliukh dlia vechirky

snail

равлик

ravlyk

blackberry

ожина
ozhyna

currant

смородина
smorodyna

clementine

клементин
klementyn

durian

дуріан
durian

dragon fruit

пітая
pitaia

jackfruit

джекфрут
dzhekfrut

star fruit

карамболь
karambol

asparagus

спаржа
sparzha

radish

редиска
redyska

red bean

червона квасоля

chervona kvasolia

turnip

ріпа
ripa

cassava

маніок
maniok

sweet potato

Коренеплоди батату
Koreneplody batatu

chickpeas

нут
nut

eagle

орел
orel

bat

летюча миша
letiucha mysha

beaver

бобер
bober

flamingo

фламінго
flaminho

raven

ворон
voron

blackbird

дрізд
drizd

blue tit

синиця блакитна
synytsia blakytna

magpie

сорока
soroka

swallow bird

ластівка
lastivka

lark

жайворонок
zhaivoronok

parakeet

папуга
papuha

woodpecker

дятел
diatel

peacock

павич
pavych

parrot

папуга
papuha

toucan

тукан
tukan

stork

лелека
leleka

coral

корал
koral

sea anemone

морська анемона
morska anemona

sea urchin

морський їжак
morskyi izhak

seahorse

морський коник
morskyi konyk

clownfish

риба-клоун
ryba-kloun

goldfish

золота рибка
zolota rybka

crab

краб
krab

hermit crab

рак-самітник
rak-samitnyk

dolphin

дельфін
delfin

narwhal

нарвал
narval

octopus

восьминіг
vosmynih

squid

кальмар
kalmar

whale shark

китова акула
kytova akula

orca

косатка
kosatka

blue whale

синій кит
synii kyt

beluga whale

білуха
bilukha

hammerhead shark

акула-молот

akula-molot

white shark

біла акула

bila akula

lemon shark

лимонна акула

lymonna akula

tiger shark

тигрова акула

tyhrova akula

grasshopper

коник

konyk

caterpillar

гусениця

husenytsia

scorpion

скорпіон

skorpion

lizard

ящірка

iashchirka

dinosaurs

динозаври

dynozavry

black hair

чорне волосся

chorne volossia

ginger hair

руде волосся

rude volossia

brown hair

каштанове волосся

kashtanove volossia

blond hair

світле волосся

svitle volossia

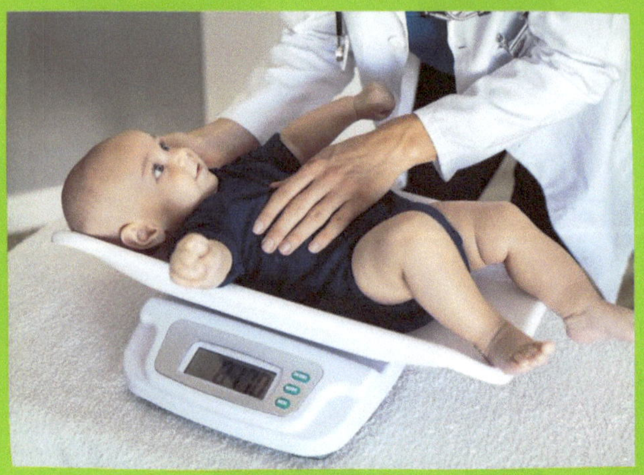

scale

ваги
vahy

hospital

лікарня
likarnia

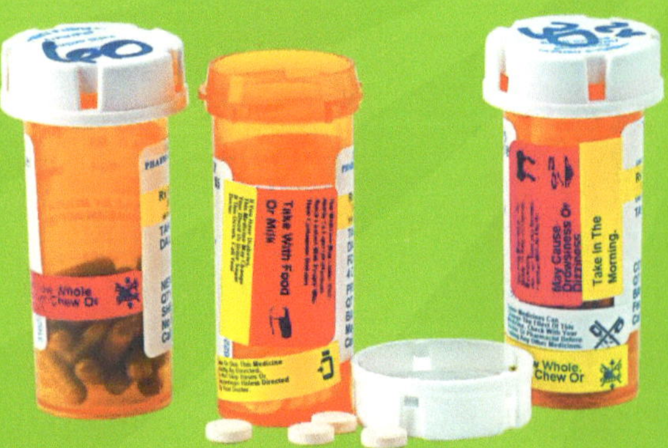

medicine

ліки
liky

thermometer

термометр
termometr

bandage

пластир
plastyr

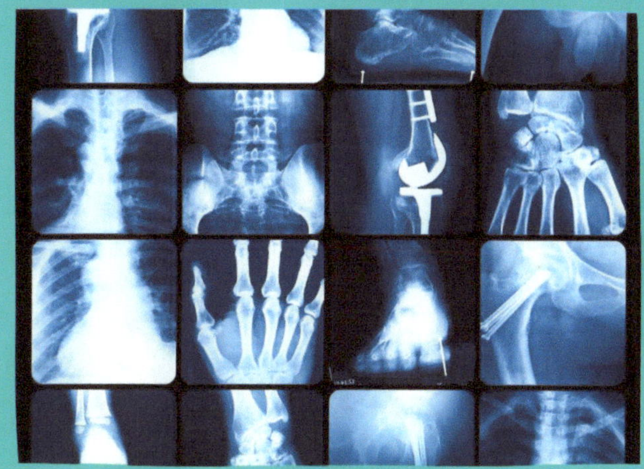

x-ray

рентген
renthen

doctor

лікар
likar

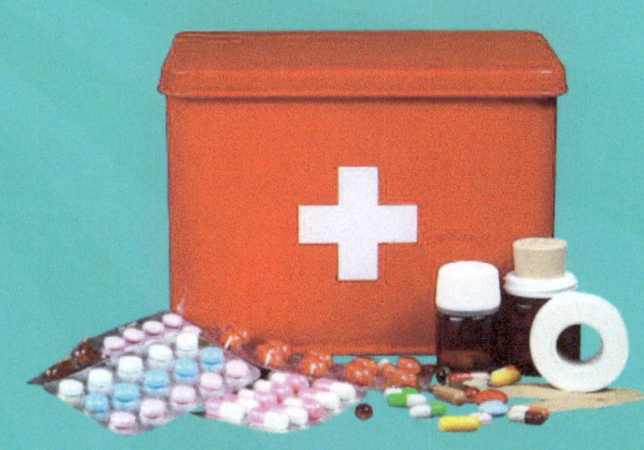

first aid kit

аптечка першої допомоги
aptechka pershoi dopomohy

play

грати
hraty

draw

малювати
maliuvaty

count

рахувати
rakhuvaty

write

писати
pysaty

dancing

танці

tantsi

swimming

плавання

plavannia

skiing

лижний спорт

lyzhnyi sport

basketball

баскетбол

basketbol

tennis

теніс

tenis

ping pong

настільний теніс

nastilnyi tenis

soccer

футбол

futbol

horse riding

верхова їзда

verkhova izda

ice hockey

хокей
khokei

judo

дзюдо
dziudo

boxing

бокс
boks

running

біг
bih

baseball

бейсбол
beisbol

cricket

крикет
kryket

rugby

регбі
rehbi

volleyball

волейбол
voleibol

maracas

маракаси
marakasy

tambourine

тамбурин
tamburyn

xylophone

ксилофон
ksylofon

violin

скрипка
skrypka

piano

фортепіано
fortepiano

guitar

гітара
hitara

cello

віолончель
violonchel

harp

арфа
arfa

drum

барабан
baraban

djembe

джембе
dzhembe

drum kit

ударна установка
udarna ustanovka

trumpet

труба
truba

horn

ріг
rih

saxophone

саксофон
saksofon

flute

флейта
fleita

headphone

навушники
navushnyky

sing

співати
spivaty

sheet music

ноти
noty

microphone

мікрофон
mikrofon